The Little
Book
of
Hope

The Little

Book

of

Hope

Meera Riitta Ojala

REGENT PRESS
Berkeley, California
2020

ISBN 13: 978-1-58790-546-9
ISBN 10: 1-58790-546-9
Library of Congress Catalog Number: 2020948299

Manufactured in the U.S.A.
REGENT PRESS
Berkeley, California
www.regentpress.net

Table of Contents

The Little Book of Hope

"Hope is the thing with feathers that perches in the soul and sings the tune without the words and never stops at all."

— Emily Dickinson

Life is like traveling across a vast ocean. Sometimes the weather is really beautiful and travel is smooth. Out of nowhere a storm can arise and we have to hold onto our life raft hoping not to drown.

In the middle of the storm we don't know if we will survive. Usually we rise to fight for our life fiercely.

Hope can be like a life raft.

Sometimes it's hard to keep hope alive when we are in the middle of challenges.

Hope is an energy that makes us put one foot in front of the other, even if we feel tired or want to give up.

Hope is Light. If we are challenged, like we all are at times, Hope can bring light in. If we receive "bad news" like a difficult health diagnosis from a doctor, hope can remind us that anything is possible. Doctor's words are one reality; it's still possible for us to heal. Hope can move the fear aside and bring the Light in. It does not mean being in denial or not listening to the doctor's orders, it means making space for all possibilities, bringing Light to any situation.

In order to cultivate Hope, you don't need evidence. You need the power of your heart and soul to invite the Light in.

Hope is seeing light in the middle of darkness.

Hope is looking forward.

Hope is a seed that manifests positive things.

Hope is a state of mind where we can see positive outcomes even when we don't know how or when.

Hope can lift our gaze up to look at the future with trust and confidence.

Hope is believing that things will work out even if we don't know how.

Hope is finding courage to keep moving forward.

Hope is a Light in the heart. My wish is that this book inspires you in all aspects of your life. May the Spark of Hope guide you on your journey!

"Hope is the companion of power, and mother of success; for who so hopes strongly has within him the gift of miracles."

— Samuel Smiles

My Story

A few months after my mother and father died (3 months apart from each other), I received a cancer diagnosis. It was like a rug had been pulled from underneath my feet. It was a total shock, like an earthquake. I couldn't feel the ground under my feet anymore. Life was not the same as minutes before the doctor had given me the news.

It felt like having cancer meant death. I had literally just received a death sentence. I wondered how much longer I had to live. I felt great sadness thinking about my loved ones and that I would not be with them anymore.

Fear was like a big mountain blocking me from seeing anything else. My head was spinning. I couldn't begin to understand that this was actually happening to me. It was a huge shock. Tears were streaming down my cheeks. I felt totally lost.

I don't remember how long I was in a state of shock because time stood still, and I don't remember how we got home. I don't remember much about that day at all. I remember that the next day I knew I needed to start researching about my cancer and my options. I felt deeply sad, but I needed to start taking action. I needed to understand more about my condition and my chances of survival. I researched the treatments my doctor had prescribed. It was all very scary and overwhelming.

Being present with my body and noticing the sensations helped me deal with the shock. Breath was my very good friend. Taking deep breaths helped to calm my nervous system. Listening to my body helped me track experiences in the moment; this helped me decide what I needed to do to take care of myself. Connecting with my body helped me connect to my feelings as well.

I was so afraid. The fear caused me to have a high level of anxiety. I couldn't sleep, which was not helpful at all. I asked myself, "How can I cope with this fear?" In my long practice of meditation, I had learned to witness my thoughts, to watch them like they were a movie and to understand that I was more than my thoughts. Now I applied the skill of witnessing and was able to witness my fear in a different way. This practice was a lifesaver for me during my journey with cancer. The severe physical pain was hard to witness, but witnessing created some distance to the pain. When I had to go through treatments that were scary and oftentimes painful, I witnessed my feelings and sensations.

The most important of all was witnessing the drama of me being a "cancer patient," seeing deeper that I am more than a cancer patient. Remembering that I am on this journey of spirit and even if my body is going through something difficult and challenging, my spirit will not be hurt by it. Actually, the spirit gets stronger when it goes through something challenging. When one goes through the dark night of the soul, the spirit gets "polished." It's like a diamond that gets more beautiful.

Remembering the spiritual perspective was very important for me. It didn't mean that I still wasn't afraid of death.

I did not conquer my cancer alone. Yes, I worked hard. I did my best to take care of myself and not lose hope. The wonderful support from my family and friends was important. In the end, I feel it was

God's Grace that determined that I survived. But I had to do my part.

Experiencing Loss of a Loved One or Loss of Health

*"Being willing to receive help
gives other people the gift of giving."*

Every loss is different, but there are also some similarities.

There is grief when we lose something. It can be hard to deal with the feelings associated with grief. Sometimes it feels easier to just bury them deep inside. But that will just end up hurting us in the long run. It's important to make space for our feelings, to get support and find hope in the middle of it all. Also, it's vital to find people that can be available to listen to you, to be present for you, to support you.

It's sometimes hard but important to be honest with oneself. To ask "what am I feeling?," "what kind of support do I need?" It's courageous to be willing to be vulnerable. Being willing to receive help gives other people the gift of giving. Can we open ourselves to receive help? There is no reason to be afraid to ask for help.

After a loss, life is not the same. When our loved one dies, we miss them unconsolably. After an illness we miss the healthy body we had. We might feel emotionally wounded.

There is no medicine or quick fix for the grief. It's like surfing through the rough waters. When we mourn, we are allowing ourselves to surf the waves of grief instead of fighting against them. Feeling the pain, letting tears flow and mourning the loss can feel like an unbearable journey. We might feel we are forever lost to the bottom of the darkness. But if we can allow the pain to break our hearts open, we will find a new deeper connection to ourselves and to life.

Hope is the energy that gives us courage to stay on the surfboard, continuing the ride, even when we are scared and want to give up. We emerge to the shore stronger and wiser after the wild and scary ride.

When we keep hope alive and visualize a brighter tomorrow, we are paving the road for change.

Losing something can be a wake up call and an invitation to transformation.

Spirituality

When we go through difficult challenges in life, having some kind of spiritual belief is helpful. If we can connect to something bigger than us, if we can feel that there is something more than material reality, then our perspective on life events can be different. We might be following one of the world's beautiful religions or we might have found our own connection to the Divine.

People relate in very different ways to the word "God."
For some people, God is a very particular figure. For some, it is a higher power. Something that is bigger than the individual, which could be nature, the sun, the sky or even a tree.

For some people God is the Power of Love. Power that can make us do things we would otherwise never be able to do. Like when a mother lifts up a car to save her child from underneath the car. Normally she would never be able to do it, but the power of love gives her extraordinary strength.

I believe that God, Spirit or Love is in all of us. If we connect with this Divine energy, we can feel it inside of us and in other people. Sometimes the Divine energy is covered with pain or anger or hiding behind sadness. If we can find love in our hearts and connect from love to others, we can find the Divine nature inside of them as well. "God" could mean the love and compassion that lives in all our hearts, our Buddha nature. We might not always feel it, but it is there. Bringing our awareness from the head to the heart can help connecting to the love energy.

Connecting with the Divine can happen through different channels and experiences for different people. For many people praying or devotion are ways to connect with God or the Divine. For some people physical practices can be the vehicle to connect with the Divine, for others it can happen through meditation or focusing on the breath. Some people gain understanding of the Divine through studying spiritual texts and through intellectual inquiry.

We are all spiritual beings inside this human body. There is more than just the physical world.

Bringing in the spiritual aspect is an invitation to connect to all the layers of life. Beyond the physical, emotional and mental layers there are also energetic and spiritual layers. Challenges in life can be a way to connect to these deeper layers, to discover more about ourselves.

If the word "God" does not work for you, please consider replacing it with "Divine " or "Higher Power" or "Spirit."

We all have different relationships with different words.

Allow yourself to find a word that works for you.

To the Reader

You can read this book in the order of the pages or you can just open the book anywhere trusting that you will get the most supportive message for that particular day.

I am inviting you to take a deep breath and feel your body before you start reading so you are more open to receiving the message. After reading the page it's helpful to give yourself a moment to sit and feel deeply the message you just read. Pause and do nothing. Feel your breath and your body. You might have emotions come up or physical sensations arise. Is your breathing deeper? Is your stomach relaxed or tight? How do you feel around your heart center?

Reading this book can be a journey to discover about yourself as well as to get support to ensure you are not alone in dealing with your challenges.

Allow yourself also to pause after each picture.

Pause is pregnant with possibilities. Pause can give you a chance to be aware of what is really going on in your heart, in your head and in your body. Awareness is the first step to change and growth.

I invite you to try the practices at the end of the book. These practices can be helpful in turning the pain into personal growth. I recommend that you try each of them a couple times to get a feeling for how they might assist you. After that you might choose one or two modalities to practice daily to get deeper.

Some of my writings are poems that burst out of my heart just like a volcanic eruption. Some of the writings are more philosophical, conversational investigations.

Thank you for joining me on this journey to different landscapes, mountain tops of beauty, valleys of grief, waterfalls of tears, fields of dark lava, rivers of joy, horizons of golden sunsets; it's all part of the beautiful and challenging adventure of life.

Let's live, learn, grow and evolve together.

Why Am I Writing?

I am writing to express my feelings,
I am writing so I can cleanse myself,
I am writing so more joy can flow through my body,
I am writing so I can communicate with God,
I am writing to connect with my Soul,
I am writing in order to learn about myself and life,
I am writing to share my heart with you.

Travel

Traveling on the ocean of life.
Rooted deep into the earth.
Reaching to the Light.
Radiating Love.
In the center,
there is always Peace
if you just remember to go there.
Enjoy the Joyful ride.
Celebrating life every moment.
Traveling with Peace and Trust.

Open The Door

Open the door to the space of your
True Being,
To your Essence,
Your Spirit.
To the space beyond illusions
of who you think you are.
Beyond body and mind.
Open the door to the Space of Being,
Space of relaxation,
Space of Light.
Open the door to your Soul Space.
Allow yourself to embrace your True Self.

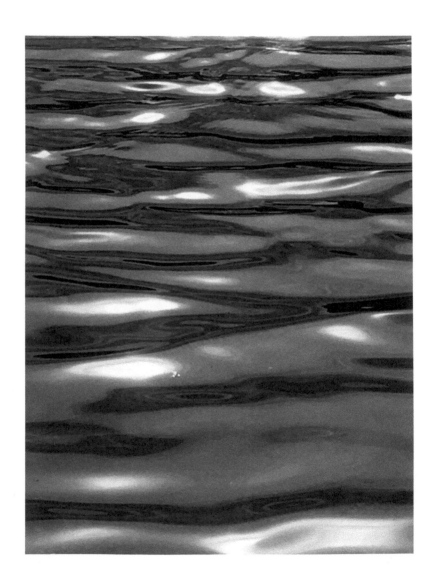

Water

Water is life.
When my body gets into the water,
whether it is river, lake, ocean,
pool or a bath tub,
it feels deeply nurtured.
It is like coming home.
Water was our first home for 9 months.
We are made of water.
We need water to survive.
Let the waters of life nurture you.

Alone

Aloneness is a part of life.
It does not need to mean loneliness,
they are different.
I am alone with myself,
the naked relationship with myself.
Nobody between me and myself.
Alone with myself.
Facing myself without masks
in the raw light of aloneness.
No make up to cover the raw feelings of
how I can not count on anybody else
but myself and God.
People come and go, meetings and departures
happen, connections are made, good byes are said.
I am still here with myself sorting out who I am, and
how to continue this journey called life Alone,
with myself and God.

Naked Presence

Two wounded souls who are protecting themselves from each other by holding shields.

They feel they need protection just in case the other one tries to hurt again like what happened in the past.

Maybe they could try to find the courage to forgive the past?

Would it be possible to be here and now without the shields?

To stand naked and vulnerable
in front of each other.

To be open to each other and
let go of the fear of getting hurt.

To be present to each other.
Here and now.
No past.
No hurt.
Just here and now.

Meditation

If we can just follow our breath and quiet our
minds, we might experience
a moment of deep joy.

If our mind is still busy,
we can witness that these are our thoughts or
feelings, only thoughts or feelings.
It is not who we really are.
We are a Spirit beyond our mind and body.

Meditation helps us to gain this larger
perspective.

Grief

When grief comes, listen.
Stay present with it.
It can be an important visitor.
Honor it, befriend it.
If we respect and listen to it,
it will leave at its own time.
It might have an important message for us.

Open Heart

Can we keep the heart open and Love flowing no matter what happens to us or around us?

Can we allow Love to be our daily nutrient for ourselves as well as those around us?

Can we return to Love even when someone has hurt us?

Can we forgive them so we can be at peace and keep our heart open?

When our heart wants to close off, we can notice it and remember that we have a choice.

If we keep our hearts open, we are happier and we bring happiness to life around us.

Nature

Being in nature is healing.
Feeling the ground beneath you,
listening to the happy chirping of the birds,
the wind dancing on the leaves of the trees,
clouds sailing by, sounds of the water.
Nature can hold you and love you
just as you are.
Let yourself be open
to receive nature's healing.

Light

Sunlight reflecting on the water.
Sunlight on the leaves of the plants.
Sunlight warming my skin.
Sunlight inside me.
God's light in me.
God's light in the world.
We are all light!

Silence

Silence feels like a cloud
that forms around me.
A cloud that supports me to relax, to let go of
my mind and the racing thoughts.
I can surrender, I am safe!
The silence can carry me
closer to my true Self.
The silence brings Peace and Joy.
Silence is a door to the Divine,
just waiting to be opened.

Light & Darkness

Sun comes out in the morning
bringing us Light.
After the sunset, Darkness comes and
takes over until the next morning.
It's the natural cycle of Light and Dark.
The same thing happens in our lives.
Sometimes it can feel like the
Darkness hovers over us for too long.
The Light will come back at some point.

Thankfulness

I am so thankful for ...

My eyes; so I can see nature's beauty, the smile of my beloved.

My ears; so I can hear the laughter of a baby, beautiful music.

My legs; so I can stand up and walk from place to place.

My hands; so I can shake hands, touch, and caress.

My brain; so I can plan things, solve problems, understand others' speech.

Compassion

When we see a person in grief, we often want to brush off their grief because we are uncomfortable feeling their suffering.

Instead, we could be present with this person's suffering and feel compassion towards them. That will bring peace and ease suffering for the grieving person as well as for ourselves.

If we understand that suffering is part of life, we can accept it and be with it. Feeling compassion allows us to open our heart.

Losing a Loved One

We miss the loved ones that have passed away.

We might get angry and depressed asking:
"Why did they have to go away?"

Yes, they are gone and yet
they will always live on in our hearts.

Because love lives forever and
love keeps them alive in our hearts.

That love also nurtures us
so we can appreciate our lives and the
Gift of life itself.

Fear

Fear can feel overwhelming. It makes our mind anxious and the body rigid. We fear things may or may not happen, but those are just thoughts in our mind causing our body to react and become tense. Fearful thoughts don't offer solutions to our problems, they just create more suffering. With the help of breath, meditation, and prayer we can release the fear, relax the body, and return to the present moment.

"I am here, I am alive, let go and let God."

Breath

Breath is Peace.
Breath is Power.
Breath is my friend, a bridge to God.
Breath is a prayer and meditation.
Every breath is a blessing.
Every breath is light.
I feel my breath.
I feel my heart beat.
I am here, fully present.

Horizon

When we look at the horizon on the ocean, it looks like it will continue for eternity. We know that at some point, we will find a shoreline if we travel across it.

Our life is like the ocean. We don't see the end of it, but at some point we will arrive at the shore, the end of our life. How are we preparing for this final landing? What skills are we acquiring so our landing will be smooth and successful? Will we be alone in this final landing?

Maybe we should prepare for this final part of our trip.

Pain

Nobody likes pain.

We all want to turn our backs to the pain and run away.
Usually that does not work. The pain follows us, until we
listen to it, until we befriend it. Just like a crying child
needs the mother to tend to them to calm them down,
similarly the pain asks for our attention.

If we resist the pain, it is more likely to persist.
If we ignore a crying child, it will cry louder and louder.
Pain can get louder and louder to get our attention.
So instead, can we listen to our pain?
Can we slow down and be present with it?
Listening to the pain, not pushing it away?
Breathing deeply, inviting softening, giving it attention.

What is the pain trying to say?
What does it need to be able to calm down?

Can we be friends with this pain?
Can we sit down and have a talk with the pain?
The pain can be an important messenger speaking for
the body's and soul's needs.

Can we slow down and listen to our pain?

Challenges

Life gives us challenges.
It's not God's intention to torture us.
We all need lessons in life in order to learn.
It's up to us how we respond to challenges.
Do we become suffering victims or
do we remember we are God's children
learning lessons?
Our Spirits are polished in the school of life.

Focus

What I focus on makes a difference
in how my day goes.

If I focus on my body feeling sick and weak,
I will feel sick and weak.

If I focus on my Spirit being strong,
it will give me strength
to move forward in my day in a positive
manner.

I can find a part of me that feels strong
to guide me forward.

I can focus on the big and small
miracles in my life.
What I focus on will grow.

Change

Change is often scary.
We are stepping into the unknown.
It can feel like walking on thin ice.
We might get across the lake,
or we might fall into the ice cold water.
We can choose to sit on the shore and wait for the
spring, thinking swimming across the lake might
be easier.

Maybe it will be.

We can resist the change and become
a dried lifeless tree on the shoreline.
Life is a river of changes, can we allow ourselves to
go with the flow and accept that nothing is
permanent?

This is hard.

We want security, we want things our way.
Yet, we cannot change the world.
We can only change ourselves, our minds,
our emotions, our expectations.

Rainbow

Rainbows bring joy to the world.
We all love the beauty of rainbows.
It takes the dark rain and bright sunlight
to create those vibrant colors.
In our lives we have both,
dark stormy days, as well as bright sunny days.
If we can love every moment
and accept any weather
– embrace the light and the dark –
we can become colorful rainbows
bringing joy to the world.

Emotions

Like weather, emotions change quickly.
Out of nowhere a storm of anger can arise.
Clouds of sadness can blow in in seconds.
The wind of anxiety can try to beat us down.
Let's just keep watching the weather,
feeling the weather,
remembering it's just the weather,
it's always changing.
We are not the weather.

Happiness

Happiness comes from the source inside of us. We can try to look for it outside of us - from money, relationships, power, and all kinds of things. But happiness from the outside can be gone at any moment, whereas happiness from the inside is always with us. When we get beyond the clouded thoughts and fears, we can find our spring of happiness inside of us. If we connect with it and keep it open, it will bubble. Then we are the happiness.

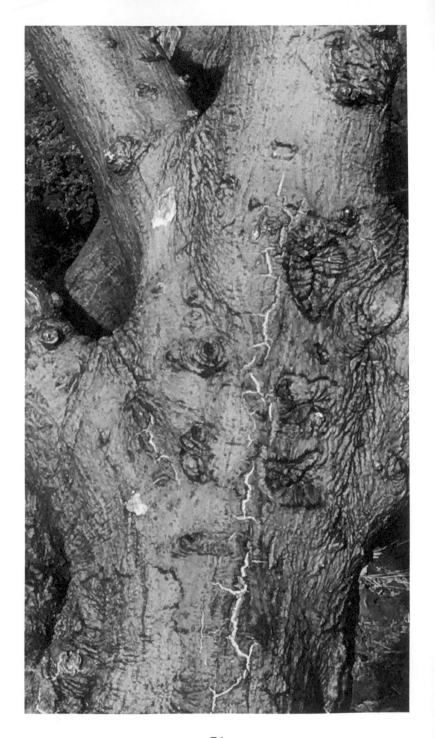

Life Will Return

I am a barren aspen tree
in the middle of winter,
feeling gray and lifeless.
But wait, someone reminded me that
soon spring will come,
and new vibrant green buds will emerge.
Life will return.
I need to remember
in the middle of winter,
when I feel gray and lifeless,
that after winter, spring will come.
Life will return.

God's Love

I have worked so hard, done my best,
and still have not reached my goal.
I have asked for help
and I am still not where I had hoped to be.
It's time to quiet down for deep prayer.
Dialing a direct line for God,
sharing my grief and worries.
Soon I start to feel God's love filling me,
and peace coming over me.
I am taken care of, I am not alone.
I am being filled with Light inside and out.
Bathed in Love and Light.

Seed of Hope

It's a miracle how from a tiny seed
a huge tree grows.
In a similar way, from one drop of Hope
a stream of Hope develops,
which grows to a river of Hope
that leads to an Ocean of Possibilities,
where small and big miracles can arise from.

Hope is a seed to a new future.
An open mind is a fertile soil for the seed.
Loving thoughts and prayers
are the nurturing rain drops.

Clouds

If you watch the white clouds
moving in the blue sky,
you will notice how they
change their shape constantly.
They create one formation and they
dissolve into a new formation.
I wish I could flow from one life situation to
another that smoothly - when an old formation
dissolves, I could trust that a new formation
will form effortlessly.
Whether it's a change in relationships, jobs,
finances, health or other circumstances, I can
trust that the Divine winds
will take me to the next place.

Dance

Feel your feet on the ground. They are there for you, supporting your whole body. Thank your feet for the big job they are doing, by carrying you around all day. Even if they are weak now, wiggle them and say hello. Do you still have five toes? Move them with the music. Let the knees and hips move. Allow the torso to circle, jiggle or roll. Bring the arms and hands to move and the head will follow. Let the music or your breath inspire further movement. I am moving - there is no right or wrong way - I am moving, I am alive!

Peace

Peace can come with presence.
Being present in the moment.
Feeling my breath,
Feeling my heart beat,
I am here,
fully present in the moment.
I am peaceful.

Heaviness

Sometimes feelings make us
feel very heavy at heart.
We can greet those feelings,
acknowledge that they are there,
but we don't need to carry them around.
We can let them go, leave it to God,
to a Higher Power, to Nature.
Breathing in Lightness,
releasing the Heaviness.

Soul Song

What is your soul singing?
Is it singing songs of joy?
Is it singing songs of longing?
Is it laughing?
Is it crying?
Is it longing to do something bigger,
something more meaningful?
Is it happy with each moment?
Is it unwaveringly content with what is?
Is it striving to grow?
Is it wanting to be closer to the Divine?
Listen to your soul's song.
Listen to what it is telling you.
Listen and then sing the song of your soul.

Heart Broken

When your heart hurts, what do you do?
You can try to run away from it or you can try to distract
yourself with drugs, alcohol,
or harmful behaviors.
To stay with your broken heart,
to feel your sadness, that is an act of courage.
Bravery is to give yourself permission to weep
and allow the waterfall of grief to open.
To feel the heart quivering of sadness,
like you were an autumn leaf
that is banged around by the wind.
Sometimes the heart can feel as heavy as a rock.
Just keep breathing into your heart,
it will get lighter.
The tears will be cleansing to your heart,
and the world will start to look brighter.
Even when the heart is hurting and you feel like it's
breaking, keep breathing love and peace into your heart.
Even if your heart breaks, keep it open and it will get bigger
and your love will flow more freely.

Breathing in peace and love.

Butterfly

Coming out of a cocoon,
With my new butterfly wings,
I am feeling tender and small.
I am not the same as I used to be.
But I am learning to fly first slowly,
Soon soaring to heights,
Flying towards freedom.
Thank you God for my wings!

Who Am I?

Who am I?
This question has been asked
for thousands of years.
If we are not our bodies or our minds,
who are we?
We can create answers in our mind,
but can we really feel the true essence
of who we really are?
We might find names like "Spirit,"
"Self," "Divine Being," "Light," or "God."
Can we really feel that
deep Truth of who we are?

Oneness

Sometimes I feel so alone.
I tell myself it's just a feeling
since I know that we are connected to all.
But some days I just can't feel the
connectedness.
Today I was floating in a tide pool,
my ears underneath the water.
I could hear my breath
and at the same time hear the ocean waves.
I felt connected to myself and
one with the ocean.
What a relief to actually *feel*
that God is in all of us and we are all one.

Expectations

We all have so many expectations. We hope to achieve this or that. We hope people will behave in certain ways toward us. We hope people are kind to us, instead they are sometimes angry. We expect them to share our values.

Yet people have acquired their own values. They communicate differently than we expected, express themselves differently. Our expectations lead us to the trap of disappointment. We are trapped in feeling sad and disappointed. We suffer. We know we don't control the world, yet we expect things to happen according to our wishes.

We can't change the world, but we can change our thoughts and expectations. We can watch life and its surprises like it's a movie. Sometimes movies end differently than we expected and we don't get too upset, we get surprised. We might say "Oh, that was interesting!" Can we do the same with life and just say: "Oh, that was interesting!" "I didn't expect that!" "That was surprising!"

It doesn't mean we have to accept injustice. We can follow the guidance of the Serenity Prayer: "God, grant me the serenity to accept the things I cannot change, Courage to change the things I can, And wisdom to know the difference.

Waves

Watching the waves.
Each wave is unique, big or small.
They roll into the shore, they roll back out.
The big waves roll further up to the shore,
but they still roll back to the ocean
just like the small waves.
They are individual waves, and yet
each one is a part of the ocean.
The waves are one with the ocean.
We humans journey through life thinking we are
alone, when in fact we are connected to everything.
If we understood this,
we would not hurt each other.
We would not destroy Mother Nature.
Understanding the Oneness brings
harmony, respect and peace.
Listen to your breath, listen to the waves,
listen to your heartbeat.
We are all one.

Dolphins

I watch how dolphins jump
happily out of the ocean.
So much joy!
They always swim together in the group.
They protect each other and
keep each other company.
We humans could learn a lot
from dolphins.
The joy of lightness and leaping!
Supporting each other, being together.
We humans try to be better than others
and instead become isolated islands.
Could we just love and play more?

Weary of Life

We all get bruised, tired and weary.
Life is a bumpy ride.
Even if we are wear seatbelts
and drive carefully,
behind every curve there could be
a deep ditch that we fall into.
How can we stay optimistic and not lose faith?
How can we keep moving forward
even when we are bruised?
If we can keep the heart open
even when it's broken, we can
Share love,
Live love,
Be love.

Diving Invitation

How about starting a diving practice; diving deeper into who we really are? Meditation can be the spiritual diving practice. Diving deeper does not happen on your first try.

Before diving in the ocean, we need to develop skills and practice with a teacher. Similarly, in meditation we need a teacher and to practice so we can learn to go deeper and deeper to discover the treasure hidden in the deep waters - our True Self.

We can start practicing by quieting our minds from all the chatter, descending down through the layers of who we think we are, and letting go of those attachments.

Then we can find a
Place of Quiet,
Place of Being,
Place of Peace,
There we find Bliss,
That is who we really are,
Blissful Soul

Mirror

I look at myself in the mirror.
I see my eyes that are very familiar,
I see wrinkles that remind me of my age.
I see the color of my hair,
I see the shape of my face.
What about inside of me?
Can I see that part of me?
My life story, my experiences, my beliefs,
my energy, my soul.
So often we focus on the outside physical reality,
which is only a small part of who we are. The unseen
reality is more powerful:
energies, mystical forces, God's symphony,
whatever you prefer to call it.

How do we tune into the unseen
to reveal that which the mirror will not show us?
What is the Truth and what is not the Truth?
The wise one knows what is important
and focuses on that.

I Have a Choice

I have a choice in every situation;
Whether to contract or to stay open,
To get angry or stay curious,
To choose hate or love,
To judge or feel compassion,
To embrace or to push away,
To accept or resist.
I have a choice.

Healing

What does it take to really heal our wounds?
When we get a cut we try to clean it,
maybe bandage it.
If it doesn't heal, we might need medicine.
When we are emotionally hurt,
part of the cleaning is expressing
our feelings about the hurt.
But how long do we need to keep cleaning?
Expression can become a swamp of anger
where we get lost. What will help the scab
to form sealing our wound?
Maybe it's forgiveness.
We understand that someone
did something wrong,
but if we stay angry it will only hurt us more.
Anger stops the wound from sealing,
and rumination creates infection,
but forgiving is medicine.

Morning

When you wake up what is your first thought?
What if you said,
"How wonderful I have another day to
experience life!" and smiled a big smile.
What if you welcomed the new day
with an open heart and
found something to be grateful for:
family, friends, pet, the morning sky, a flower.
If you allow your body and mind
to tune into the gratitude channel,
you can surf the happy waves
all day long and leave the
static worry channel behind you.

The Future

Questions unanswered
Future unknown
Faith my companion, Trust my friend
Somehow things will work out
even if we have no idea how
Unknown scares us
We can make all sorts of plans,
but there is no guarantee
that they happen the way we planned.
The future is the land of unknown
It's a mirage we try to grasp on
The best way to prepare for the future
is to be fully present in this moment.
If we find our truth in this moment
and make the best choices while
enjoying this moment,
all is going to be well.
Trusting the truth in this precious moment.

Love

We seek love and attention from people
throughout our lives
We want to feel loved so we do not feel alone
Yet, we are always alone and never alone
If we can feel that we are the Love,
we are never alone
Our open heart connects with everything
Finding the Source of Love
inside ourselves brings Peace
We are the never-ending spring of Love
Then every action arises from Love

Sleepless

Noisy thoughts filling my head,
worrying, wondering, planning...
Sleep is far away.
Until I bring my attention to my friend,
my breath.
Breathing deeply, breathing out all thoughts,
making space for silence.
Breathing out tension,
making space for more silence.
Finally the space inside my mind is
filled with silence.
Thank you silence, which brings me peace.
Now sleep can arrive.

Laughter

Laughter is healing.
Watch children and laugh
at their sweet silly playing.
Watch a comedy that brings you laughter.
Laugh at yourself
when you do something silly.
Laugh so your belly shakes
like a little earthquake,
lifting all the weight of worries away.

Music

Music is healing.
Whether it is listening to your favorite music,
or singing or playing music,
it all moves your energy.
Let music enter your heart and cleanse it.

Perspective

Even if worries or grief are a
weight on your shoulders,
lift your heart toward the sun,
see the sky, the treetops, the mountaintop.
Keep things in perspective,
see the bigger picture.

Roadblock

A roadblock does not mean
that we need to stop.
It might be just a little detour
or a curve on the road.
We need to slow down
since we can't see what's behind the curve,
but the road still continues.

Being Brave

Being brave does not mean
that you need to have a stiff upper lip
and pretend that everything is fine.
Being brave is being honest with yourself.
What am I feeling?
What is my truth?

Turbulence

A turbulent mind is a burden.
It robs us of the peace and joy of life.
Clean the mind from worries and fears
and sail the smooth skies!

Being Grateful

Life is a gift.
Challenges come,
but being alive is still a gift.
Being alive, things can change,
we can grow, we can learn!
Attitude of gratitude
will free us to enjoy life.

Struggle

Why do we struggle so much?
We fill our heads with worries,
we are anxious, we can't sleep.
When instead, we could trust
that God will take care of us.
We need to put in our best effort
to move forward
and then pray for God's Grace.

Life Raft/Life Vest

Find something bigger than you,
God, Great Spirit, as your life raft.
Something you can hold on to
when you feel like you are drowning.

Bittersweet

When you love somebody so deeply
that your heart is filled with your love
toward that person – what a blessing that is!
But then one day you had to say goodbye
to that person – what a devastating loss!
Rivers of tears flow,
pain in the heart aches and burns.
The grief is all consuming
You ask God
"Why did this have to happen?"
No answer.
Maybe after enough tears and enough time,
the pain will start to loosen its grip.
Maybe the clouds of grief will start to dissipate.
After all, the beautiful love is still there!

Inner Happiness

Nourish your heart.
What nourishes your heart?
Listen to what your heart is yearning.
Love yourself.
You can let go of your worries
and be carefree like a child.
Allow yourself to play and be in joy.
It's your birthright to live in Love and Joy.
To be free to be you.
Every cell dancing with Love and Joy.

PRACTICES

Tracking Your Body Sensations

Take a deep breath and quiet your mind so you can be present with your body sensations.

Notice how your body feels while you are reading or after you have read a page. Your body can assist you to get in touch with your true feelings behind your thoughts. Your body can be an ally in your healing journey. Please listen to your body and honor its needs.

Turning your attention to your body several times during the day will help you start to connect more with what is going on in your body. Pause from whatever you are doing, take a deep breath and get in touch with your body.

Meditation

It can be important to have a teacher to guide you in meditation and breathing practices since these can be powerful practices that can affect your mind and body in very profound ways.

Meditation helps us create a different relationship with ourselves, the world, and people around us. It allows us to experience a larger perspective, to understand that we are more than our thoughts and our mind. Meditation has been proven to benefit our physical, emotional, and spiritual health. Relaxation, peace of mind, and increased clarity and focus are some benefits.

There are multiple meditation techniques. What they all have in common is the goal of calming the mind. It's recommended that your spine be straight when you meditate. Eyes can be closed or gazing downward.

In many techniques you focus on your breath. You can say quietly with your in-breath" I am breathing in" and with your out-breath " I am breathing out." You can also repeat a mantra with each breath. A mantra can be a simple word of what you want to invite into your life like "peace" or it can be a Sanskrit word, or names of the Divine. You can also sit in silence just observing your breath. If thoughts arise you can bring your attention back to the breath.

Instead of coming back to your breath, you can also witness your thoughts with awareness. You can label the thought and witness part of your mind labeling the thoughts. Thoughts arise and dissipate, we don't need to be caught in them. Learning to stay grounded as a witness when emotions arise helps us not to be hijacked by them. The only thing that does not change is the witnessing awareness. You can't force your mind to quiet, but you can cultivate moments of quiet that can grow longer and longer. Gradually this peace will extend beyond your meditation time.

Breathing Exercises

There are a multitude of breathing exercises from different traditions. Breathing is a very powerful way to change our physical, emotional, and energetic states.

A good place to start is to connect to our regular every day breathing. How is our breath flowing? To which parts of the body? How fast? Is there a difference between the length of the in-breath and out-breath? Just paying attention to our breath helps us to feel more centered and grounded.

When we are anxious or fearful, taking a deep belly breath is very helpful. It will shift our nervous system to a calm parasympathetic state.

If we are depressed we need to do active breathing and that will energize us. A very common and very old breathing practice that comes from Yoga tradition is an Alternate Nostril breathing. If it's done slowly it can be calming. When done faster it will be energizing. Please be mindful about the speed. Too fast (like rapid panting) can cause hyperventilation and be harmful physically or emotionally.

Here is how to do Alternate Nostril Breathing:

1. Take a comfortable seat, sit up nice and tall making sure your spine is straight and your heart is open.
2. Relax your left palm comfortably into your lap and bring your right hand just in front of your face.
3. With your right hand, fold your index and middle finger in to your palm. The fingers we'll be actively using are the thumb and ring finger.
4. Close your eyes and take a deep breath in and out through your nose.
5. Close your right nostril with your right thumb. Inhale through the left nostril slowly and steadily.

6. Close the left nostril with your ring finger so both nostrils are held closed; retain your breath at the top of the inhale for a brief pause.

7. Open your right nostril and release the breath slowly through the right side; pause briefly at the bottom of the exhale.

8. Inhale through the right side slowly.

9. Hold both nostrils closed very briefly (with ring finger and thumb).

10. Open your left nostril and release breath slowly through the left side. Pause briefly at the bottom.

11. Repeat 5-10 cycles, allowing your mind to follow your inhales and exhales.

12. Expand the practice gradually.

Yoga

Yoga is much more than physical stretches. Yoga is a philosophy that is too large to fully describe here.

Yoga helps us to awaken to who we truly are. The Sanskrit word "Yoga" means union. The diversity of practices in yoga can help unite us with the higher consciousness. Another definition for Yoga is "to be one with the Divine." It does not matter what Divine is for us (God, Allah, or anything else). Yoga is believing and connecting with the Higher Power greater that us.

The **eight limbs of Yoga** are: yama (abstinences), niyama (observances), asana (Yoga postures), pranayama (breath control), pratyahara (withdrawal of the senses), dharana (concentration), dhyana (meditation) and samadhi (absorption).

Many people in the West think of Yoga as a physical practice, which is only a part of the eight limbs. Asana is the limb of Yoga where we practice the "postures" to help balance our body, mind and spirit. It's important to connect the movement and the breath. Withdrawal of the senses and concentration help us develop being observer and what is observed at the same time. We work on integration of body, breath and mind to connect with our larger Self.

In ancient times yoga was often referred to as a tree, a living entity with roots, a trunk, branches, blossoms, and fruit. Traditionally there are 4 branches in Yoga. Each branch with its unique characteristics and function represents a particular approach to life.

There are numerous styles of yoga that different teachers have developed.

There is a body of research about the many benefits of yoga for our physical, emotional, mental, and spiritual wellbeing.

Yoga Nidra is a systematic method of guiding one to physical, mental, and emotional relaxation. It is also referred as Psychic sleep or Deep relaxation with inner awareness. It's an ancient practice from India that has grown popular in the West. It has been used to treat sleep disorders, PTSD, anxiety, and many other conditions as well as enhance general wellbeing and spiritual deepening.

It is usually practiced lying down with a teacher guiding the session.
It can facilitate deep restful state (Theta state), a place where we can restructure our psychology and connect to our intuition and creativity.

Yoga Nidra works with 'sankalpa', which loosely translates to "resolve." Sankalpa is usually a short mental statement which affects the subconscious mind during the practice of Yoga Nidra. Sankalpa is like a seed that can help us make positive changes and accomplish goals.

Movement

It can be helpful to allow your body to move if you feel strong emotions and/or have physical pain. You can turn music on, slow or fast, depending on what feels right. You can be on the bed, on the floor, or on the couch. You can also move in silence just listening to your breath and your body.

Allow your body to move in just the way it wants to. There is no right or wrong way, except not doing anything that will hurt your body. Even micro-movements, like the rising and moving of your chest, are beneficial and help you to connect and express your feelings.

Journaling

When feelings come up, it can be good to write about them in your journal. Allow yourself to write freely without holding anything back. Open expression is freeing. You can have a deep conversation with yourself, or do free associative writing; writing down the flow of your thoughts, without any screening, censoring or judgment.

Journaling is also a good way to get to know yourself better. It can be a peaceful and nurturing time to be with yourself and your feelings. It is an opportunity to reflect upon your life.

Exercise

Cardiovascular movement, any kind of exercise, is not only good for the physical body, but can really stimulate the brain and lift emotions. There are many ways, like walking, biking, or swimming. Find one way that you like to exercise and just do it daily. You will see it works.

Art

Drawing your feelings can be helpful. You can try chalk pastels that mix colors easily; it makes the art experience very kinesthetic. Any colors work fine. Just get the colors out and do it!

I recommend starting with a centering exercise; closing your eyes, taking a deep breath, and feeling the body. Once centered choose a color that attracts you, no thinking needed. Start to make shapes and colors that feel right, again no thinking needed. Keep listening to your breath and your body. When you feel complete then stop to look at your picture and see if it has a story. If it had a title what would it be called?

After this you can write about your drawing, a few words, in a poem or a story. You can also prop it on the table and look at it and let your body move the story of the drawing. Very interesting journeys can unfold through this practice.

Laughter

Find funny movies or comic books or silly animal videos, something that makes you laugh even when you feel lousy. Laughter moves energy and releases tension, it is medicine. But it does not happen when we are challenged unless we seek for it consciously. Find friends to laugh with.

Visualization & Prayer

Instead of getting overwhelmed by worry we can turn to visualization or prayer. There is plenty of evidence that both of these create positive change.

You can pray to any Divine power that you relate to, asking for help, for healing.

Visualizing a good outcome or change will give energy for it to manifest. You can visualize golden light in all your cells or in your heart. You can visualize love filling you or your loved one. You can visualize a resolution scenario to a difficult situation.

Remembering Perspective & Finding Gratitude

It's good to remember that everything changes.

"Right now I am having hard time" does not mean that it will be that way forever. "This too shall pass" is very true.

Affirmation gives you comfort.

A good story about perspective is a Zen Story.

Zen Story: Maybe

There is a Taoist story of an old farmer who had worked his crops for many years. One day his horse ran away. Upon hearing the news, his neighbors came to visit. "Such bad luck," they said sympathetically. "Maybe," the farmer replied.

The next morning the horse returned, bringing with it three other wild horses. "How wonderful," the neighbors exclaimed. "Maybe," replied the old man.

The following day, his son tried to ride one of the untamed horses, was thrown, and broke his leg. The neighbors again came to offer their sympathy on his misfortune. "Maybe," answered the farmer.

The day after, military officials came to the village to draft young men into the army. Seeing that the son's leg was broken, they passed him by. The neighbors congratulated the farmer on how well things had turned out. "Maybe," said the farmer.

The farmer in this story is accepting each challenge, acknowledging that it's part of life. He takes life as it comes, without attachment. Non-attachment does not mean that we don't care. It frees us to appreciate each moment. Worrying about things will not bring positive outcomes.

What we focus on will grow. If we find things to be grateful for, we feel better than if we feel sorry for ourselves. We can always find something to be grateful for, like the fact we can breathe without pain, or that we have a friend or family, or someone said a kind word for us. Finding things to be grateful for will shift our focus toward positive thinking and cultivate hope. Keeping a gratitude journal can be a nice way to cultivate our focus on gratitude.

Relaxation Practices

There are many wonderful relaxation practices and relaxation tapes. Just listening to calming music can be very relaxing. If the body is very tense a progressive relaxation technique can be helpful in relaxing your mind and your body.

You tense and relax each muscle group one at a time, going through your entire body. If you have pain or discomfort you can skip that part of your body. It's helpful to do this with your eyes closed and lying down, but you can also do it sitting up. Most often it's done starting from your feet and moving up the body muscle group by muscle group.

Yoga Nidra is a very effective relaxation practice, see more on the section of yoga.

Sound

When in emotional stress or in physical pain, making sounds can release pain effectively. Music can be an effective tool helping us deal with difficult feelings. Music can stir feelings up helping to release them.

Making strong Ahh's and Uhh's can feel great, as well as expressing emotions with sounds. Moaning, wailing, sounding, chanting, singing are all good ways to express feelings and move energy. Joining a choir or drum circle can be life changing. Listening to our favorite music can be soothing and uplifting. Calming music helps relax the nervous system.

Spiritual Perspective or Sacredness

It's very helpful if we can feel connected to something bigger than ourselves. Having a relationship to God or the Divine can provide a feeling of support: "I am not alone on this journey." It can also help in gaining a bigger perspective into one's suffering.

If you don't have religious or spiritual beliefs you can still find something sacred in your life. Maybe it's creating a healing altar, where you have special object(s) that encourage you or support your healing. When I was sick I had a picture of a woman jumping on the beach reminding me that one day I would be able to do that too. After recovering from my second cancer I had my picture taken on the beach. I was jumping just like the woman in the picture. It was a sacred picture to me. Natural objects can have sacred and symbolic meaning. Having plants can help support our healing power.

Asking & Receiving Support

It's important to learn to ask for support and to be willing to receive it.

We are not meant to go through the challenges of life alone.

When we lose a loved one or our health, it is time to reach out for support, whether it is talking about your feelings to a friend, family member, and/or a counselor.

Even when you might feel depressed from your loss, it is good not to isolate. It can be very helpful to find a support group, either on-line or in-person, to connect with other people who are going through similar challenges.

Volunteering

When we have lost something, whether it's part of our health or a loved one, we sometimes fall into a dark hole. It is natural to withdraw after a loss and take time in silence to heal. After a certain time it can be healthy to get out and help others. This can really help us to find new meaning in our lives.

Author's Note

The journey continues. I have used all the practices I mentioned. Still after 3 years in remission, I am including some of those practices in my daily routine of self-care. I am deeply grateful to be alive. I try not to take things for granted. My intention is to love my life and myself unconditionally, even if it's not all perfect and many things in my body and in my life are different after my illnesses.

At times fears will surface. If I have an odd stomach pain and my mind says: "What is that? Do you think something is really wrong?" That is when I need to find my breath, be present with the body, to take care of the body's needs and to remember the bigger perspective.

Meditation and exercise (dance, swimming, walking, yoga) have been the most important part of my daily wellness routine. They bring so much joy; it's not just for the physical body, but also for the mind and spirit .

I have been fortunate to have a great team of both conventional and alternative health care practitioners to help my healing.

I have learned how to demonstrate commitment to live according to one's values. I am committed to being committed to my health. I feel like this helps all my cells align with my commitment to self-care and self-love.

Commitment to myself means commitment to good choices, with what and with whom I surround myself, what activities I do, what I eat, etc. From commitment grows discipline; I am choosing actions that support my health. Distractions, laziness, other peoples' critique and many other things can distract me from making good choices. I can keep choosing self-love. Out of caring for myself caring for others arises. Healing myself inspires me to support other people's healing.
Supportive family, friends and community have been important for me. Many healing practitioners

have been assets on my healing path. My spiritual teacher Amma has always been there to support and help me.

I feel like I am more deeply awake and alive now than before my illness. Loss can be an opportunity for emotional and spiritual growth. It would be nice if we could learn life's lessons without suffering, but challenges are part of life. We increase our suffering when we rebel against our challenges or assume a victim role. If we accept them, we can learn from them.

My intention is to practice being present in the moment and simply accept this moment. Even if my experience might be one of discomfort, I can find peace within it.

I hope to continue staying in love with life, caring for myself and others. It's beautiful to share the love, our life-force, to live in love and service.

"May the tree of our life be firmly rooted in the soil of love; Let good deeds be the leaves on that tree; May words of kindness form its flowers; and may Peace be its fruits." Sri Mata Amritanandamayi Devi

Recommended Books

1. *The Yamas & Niyamas, Exploring Yoga's Ethical* Practice by Deborah Adele

2. *Tuesdays with Morrie, An Old Man, A Young Man, and Life's Greatest Lesson* by Mitch Albom

3. *Bodyfulness, Somatic Practices for Presence, Empowerment, and Waking Up in This Life* by Christine Caldwell Ph.D.

4. *Taking the Leap, Freeing Ourselves from Old Habits and Fears* by Pema Chodron

5. *Invitation* by Oriah Mountains Dreamer

6. *Man's Search for Meaning* by Viktor E. Frankl

7. *Anatomy of Hope* by Jeromy Groopman

8. *Returning to Health: With Dance, Movement & Imagery* by Anna Halprin

9. *Light on Yoga* by B.K.S. Iyengar

10. *No Mud, No Lotus, The Art of Transforming Suffering* by Thich Nhat Hanh

11. *The Grief Recovery Handbook, The Action Program For Moving Beyond Death, Divorce, and Other Losses* by John W. James and Russell Friedman

12. *Broken Open, How Difficult Times Can Help Us Grow* by Elizabeth Lesser

13. *A Year to Live: How To Live This Year As If It Were Your Last* by Stephen Levine

14. *Healing Into Life and Death* by Stephen Levine

15. *To Bless the Space Between Us, A Book of Blessings* by John O'Donohue

16. *Sacred Journey* by Swamini Krishnamrita Prana

17. *From Amma's Heart, Conversations with Sri Mata Amritanandamayi Dev*, Translated and Written by Swami Amritaswarupananda Puri

18. *Sweat Your Prayers* by Gabrielle Roth

162

19. *Yoga Nidra* by Swami Satyananda Saraswati

20. *Change Me Prayers, The Hidden Power of Spiritual Surrender* by Tosha Silver

21. *The Untethered Soul, The Journey Beyond Yourself* by Michael A. Singer

22. *Hope Heals, A True Story of Overwhelming Loss and an Overcoming Love* by Katherine and Jay Wolf

23. *Awakening From Grief, Finding the Way Back to Joy* by John Welshons

24. *Understanding Your Grief, Ten Essential Touchstones for Finding Hope and Healing Your Heart* by Alan D. Wolfelt, Ph.D.

Acknowledgements

I am very thankful for my editors Suzy McIntyre and Esta Fedora and my publisher Mark Weiman at Regent Press who made it possible to publish this book.

I have been blessed to encounter and study with many wonderful teachers on my journey of healing and learning in my life. One of the most influential teachers is Christine Caldwell who has been my teacher, supervisor, and mentor for decades. Currently I am thankful to be a student of Kumu Keala Ching, learning about Hawaiian culture and hula.

I am grateful for my family and friends for all their support.

I thank my spiritual teacher Amma, Mata Amritanandamayi Devi, for all her guidance.

I thank each one of you readers for opening this book and sharing a journey together.

— Meera Riitta

Photo Credits

Most pictures are by the author, with exception of the following:

Serina Ojala
p. 34, "Naked Presence"
p. 74, "Happiness"
p. 90, "Soul Song"
p. 114, "Healing"

Seed of Hope, Unknown, p.80

Ben Lipman "Dance" p. 84

Broken Heart, LunarSeaArt from pixabay, p.92

Ryan Brennan "Dolphins" p.104

Sveta from Getty Images Signature, "Weary Wayfarer" p. 106

Christina Montalva "Diving" p.108

Okan Akdeniz "Sunrise Burst Forest" p.116

Rahul Pandit "Heart Clouds" p.120

About the Author

Exploring and helping others in integrating body, mind and spirit has been a lifelong passion for Meera Riitta. She grew up in Finland surrounded by nature that always inspired and provided healing support for her. Walking in the woods was her favorite activity in addition to dancing and doing yoga. Still every day nature brings her joy and nurturing, and dance and yoga are part of her life. Meera Riitta graduated with a master's degree from Naropa University's Somatic Psychology Program in 1998 (Boulder, CO). She worked and trained with Christine Caldwell, founder of the Moving Cycle Institute and a Department Head of the Somatic Psychology Department of Naropa University. Meera Riitta also studied with Anna Halprin creator of "The Life Art Process."

After graduating she worked in various clinical therapeutic settings using movement, art, yoga, adventure therapy and meditation as ways to bring healing. She is a Licensed Professional Counselor. She studied different healing modalities including Swedish massage, yoga, shiatsu, Ayurveda, macrobiotics and meditation, which are part of her daily practices even today. She also teaches meditation.

In 2014 she received her first cancer diagnosis, and the second one in 2017. This propelled her to dive deeper into her spiritual practices. She has been influenced by different religions and various spiritual practices and approaches.

The cancer journey became a transformative journey, a way to dive deeper into spirituality as well as clean emotional layers. Priorities in life shifted considerably.

She currently offers coaching services to support people in physical, mental, emotional and spiritual health and personal growth. She also works as a Bereavement Counselor at Hospice of Kona, in Hawaii.

For more information or to connect with Meera Riitta please go to: www.TheBalanceWorks.com